HILLSIDE PUBLIC LIBRARY

3 1992 00226 7871

JUN 19 2019

W9-ASC-728

HILLSIDE PUBLIC LIBRARY
405 N. HILLSIDE AVENUE
HILLSIDE, IL 60162
708-449-7510

TRUE TEEN STORIES

TRUE STORIES OF
Teen Refugees

Bridey Heing

Cavendish
Square

New York

Hillside Public Library

Published in 2018 by Cavendish Square Publishing, LLC
243 5th Avenue, Suite 136, New York, NY 10016

Copyright © 2018 by Cavendish Square Publishing, LLC

First Edition

No part of this publication may be reproduced, stored in a retrieval system, or transmitted
in any form or by any means—electronic, mechanical, photocopying, recording, or
otherwise—without the prior permission of the copyright owner. Request for permission
should be addressed to Permissions, Cavendish Square Publishing, 243 5th Avenue,
Suite 136, New York, NY 10016. Tel (877) 980-4450; fax (877) 980-4454.

Website: cavendishsq.com

This publication represents the opinions and views of the author based on his or her personal
experience, knowledge, and research. The information in this book serves as a general guide
only. The author and publisher have used their best efforts in preparing this book and
disclaim liability rising directly or indirectly from the use and application of this book.

All websites were available and accurate when this book was sent to press.

Cataloging-in-Publication Data

Names: Heing, Bridey.
Title: True stories of teen refugees / Bridey Heing.
Description: New York : Cavendish Square, 2018. | Series: True teen stories | Includes index.
Identifiers: ISBN 9781502631626 (library bound) | ISBN 9781502634009
(paperback) | ISBN 9781502631633 (ebook)
Subjects: LCSH: Teenage refugees.
Classification: LCC HV640.H43 2018 | DDC 362.7'7914083--dc23

Editorial Director: David McNamara
Editor: Caitlyn Miller
Copy Editor: Alex Tessman
Associate Art Director: Amy Greenan
Designer: Deanna Paternostro
Production Coordinator: Karol Szymczuk
Photo Research: J8 Media

The photographs in this book are used by permission and through the courtesy of: Cover, Romano Cagnoni/Getty Images;
Background image—crumpled paper; p. 4 Bain collection/Library of Congress/File: Syrian Children.jpg/Wikimedia
Commons; p. 8 Oxfam East Africa/(http://www.flickr.com/people/46434833@N05)/File: Oxfam East Africa - A mass
grave for children in Dadaab.jpg/Wikimedia Commons; p.12 Sadik Gulec/Shutterstock.com; pp. 14, 67 Ververidis Vasilis/
Shutterstock.com; p. 17 Free Wind/Shutterstock.com; p. 19 Patrick Aventurier/Gamma-Rapho/Getty Images; p. 25
Kencf0618, own work/File: AntiIII% Anti Anti Refugee Boisean Punk.jpg/Wikimedia Commons; p. 29 USAID/File:
Darfur IDPs 1 camp.jpg/Wikimedia Commons; p. 33 Albert Gonzalez Farran-UNAMID/Anadolu Agency/Getty Images;
p. 34 Marco Di Lauro/Getty Images; p. 37 Thomas Coex/AFP/Getty Images; p. 38 Marco Di Lauro/Getty Images; p. 41
Evelyn Hockstein/MCT/Getty Images; p.44 L. Rose/File: DRC- Child Soldiers.jpg/Wikimedia Commons; p. 47 United
States Central Intelligence Agency/File: Sudan-CIA WFB Map.png/Wikimedia Commons; p. 48 Mustafa Bader, own
work/File: A bakery shop at Al-Zaatari camp.jpg/Wikimedia Commons; p. 53 From CIA World Factbook/File: Jo-map.
png/Wikimedia Commons; p. 54 DFID - UK Department for International Development (http://www.flickr.com/
people/14214150@N02)/File: Two women walk through the Zaatari refugee camp in northern Jordan (9634884939).jpg/
Wikimedia Commons; p. 57 U.S. Department of State/File: An Aerial View of the Za'atri Refugee Camp.jpg/Wikimedia
Commons; p. 59 DFID - UK Department for International Development (http://www.flickr.com/people/14214150@
N02)/File: Refugee children from Syria at a clinic in Ramtha, northern Jordan (9613477263).jpg/Wikimedia Commons;
p. 60 Florian Gaertner/Photothek/Getty Images; p. 64 Nicolalas Economou/Shutterstock.com; p. 69 Ggia, own work/File:
20151030 Syrians and Iraq refugees arrive at Skala Sykamias Lesvos Greece 2.jpg/Wikimedia Commons; p. 72 Sorneguer,
own work/File: Diavata refugee camp greece.jpg/Wikimedia Commons; p. 74 De Visu/Shutterstock.com; p. 79 The
World Factbook 2013-14. Washington, DC: Central Intelligence Agency, 2013/File: Gr-map.png/Wikimedia Commons;
p. 80 Mstyslav Chernov, own work/File: Syrian refugees strike in front of Budapest Keleti railway station. Refugee
crisis. Budapest, Hungary, Central Europe, 3 September 2015.jpg/Wikimedia Commons; p. 83 txking/Shutterstock.
com; p. 86 udeyismail/Shutterstock.com; p. 89 Procyk Radek/Shutterstock.com; p. 93 David Rogers/Getty Images.

Manufactured in China.

CONTENTS

A Growing Crisis

Since 2015, the world has been experiencing a refugee and **migrant** crisis of unprecedented levels. The movement of millions of people, a majority of whom are fleeing **famine**, natural disaster, or war, is taking place around the globe. Thousands are forced to leave their homes each day. From Asia to Africa to Europe to North America, policy makers and humanitarian organizations are grappling with how best to help these vulnerable people while rethinking laws regulating borders and immigration.

In late 2015, the number of refugees and **displaced persons** around the world hit record levels, with an estimated 65.3 million people fleeing their homes and seeking safety elsewhere. According to the Pew Research Center, this means that around one in one hundred people are displaced. Over 23 million are formally seeking **refugee status** in countries

Opposite: Syrian children arriving in New York in 1910. Today, Syrian refugees struggle to find a place to call home.

other than their home country and more than 37 million are displaced within their home country. According to the United Nations, the number of displaced persons now is higher than the time period following World War II.

Of those over 65.3 million refugees around the world, around half are under the age of eighteen. Teenage refugees, many of whom are alone, face unique difficulties. Women and children have long made up the majority of refugee populations. Today is no different. But what has changed in the past century is our understanding of what it means to be a teenager and what unique needs teenagers have to ensure proper mental, emotional, and physical development. For many teenage refugees, however, access to basic needs like shelter and education is far from guaranteed.

Millions of refugees live in **refugee camps**, or temporary shelters set up for the purpose of housing them until **resettlement** can be finalized or they can return to their countries of origin. In some cases, such as for Palestinian refugees, returning to their homes is not an option even decades after they originally fled. Syrians, who make up the majority of refugees seeking shelter today in many parts of the world, are also unable to return to their homes. It is unclear when the civil war taking place in Syria will end, making it safe enough for them to do so. Most camps are overseen and run by the **United Nations High Commissioner for Refugees**, or UNHCR, an international organization that works with regional security forces and governments to provide for the basic needs of refugees. Many other refugees choose to live in cities, often struggling with subpar housing or homelessness and a total lack of advocacy or services.

For teenagers, whether they live in camps or in cities, life as a refugee is difficult and dangerous. Young people are vulnerable to exploitation by employers who seek to take advantage of them or adults who threaten their lives and livelihoods. Many are forced to leave school to help take care of their families or to find jobs, and thousands of young girls are forced into marriages that take them away from their families and close the door to education. Most teenagers have little control over their own lives and are instead reliant on the kindness of others and the availability of even basic resources, like access to food and water.

In this book, we will be learning about the people and organizations trying to help make sure refugees have access to what they need to thrive. We'll examine the reality of day-to-day life for teenage refugees living in Darfur, Jordan, and Greece. All come from different circumstances and have lived in camps or as refugees for differing amounts of time. Some, such as those from Syria, left behind lives that look a lot like the average teenager—with friends, sports, school, and social media—and have had to adapt to life in a camp. Others have been sent to safety by families who are still living in dangerous situations and are trying to make it on their own in a foreign country. Some of the teens we'll learn about have spent most of their lives as refugees, and they know no other life than the one they lead now. Almost all of them are dealing with **trauma** from what they have seen and experienced. All hope for a brighter future. Teenage refugees may live lives that are very different than the average teenager, but at the end of the day, these young people are just like teens anywhere: smart, strong, and full of potential.

CHAPTER ONE

Teen Refugees Today

Large migrations have been caused throughout history by phenomena like conflict, famine, persecution, and other disasters. But the term "refugee" as we understand it didn't emerge until the United Nations 1951 Refugee Convention created the legal definition for the word that we still use today:

> Owing to well-founded fear of being persecuted for reasons of race, religion, **nationality**, membership of a particular social group or political opinion, is outside the country of his nationality and is unable or, owing to such fear, is unwilling to avail himself of the protection of that country; or who, not having a nationality and being outside the country of his former habitual residence as a result of such events, is unable or, owing to such fear, is unwilling to return to it.

Opposite: A girl stands in front of a graveyard for child refugees in Kenya. Many refugees face dangerous journeys to reach safety.

That definition was expanded at a 1967 meeting to include "every person ... compelled to leave his place of habitual residence in order to seek refuge in another place outside his country of origin or nationality." Generally speaking, when we talk about refugees, we are referring to any person who has fled their country of residence and cannot return because of threats posed to their life for a variety of reasons.

Although the definition of a refugee was set in 1951, it was in 1921 that the first large-scale international efforts to assist displaced people were organized. That year, the **League of Nations** created the High Commission for Refugees to help the 1.5 million people displaced by the Russian Revolution and ongoing fighting there. Over the years, the **mandate** for the commission expanded to include Armenian, Turkish, Assyrian, and other populations that had fled conflict, persecution, and other threats.

In the 1930s, the rise of fascism in Germany and elsewhere led to widespread efforts to evacuate children and adolescents. The League of Nations oversaw multiple efforts to resettle refugees from areas controlled by Nazis in the late 1930s, as well as evacuating children from areas affected by the Spanish Civil War. Other efforts were undertaken by specific countries, like the Kindertransport that brought thousands of German Jewish child refugees to Great Britain between 1938 and 1940. In 1950, the United Nations High Commissioner for Refugees was created, and it has since overseen international aid and work with refugees.

Just as our understanding of the term refugee has evolved, so has our understanding of adolescence and childhood. For much of history, the term "teenager" wasn't in use—in fact it only came into use in the mid-twentieth century. As a result, it can be difficult to track teenage refugees through history. But children and adolescents have long been negatively affected by the kinds of events that lead to refugee populations. They are specifically at risk for exploitation, abuse, and other difficulties when forced to flee their countries of origin. This fact has not changed today. Many are separated from their parents and forced to navigate a new country on their own while finding ways to take care of themselves in societies that can be hostile toward them. The UNHCR states that in 2015, around 98,400 **unaccompanied children** filed asylum applications, a record high since the organization started collecting data in 2006.

WHERE REFUGEES COME FROM

The majority of refugees around the world come from just three countries. Nearly five million come from Syria, where a civil war has raged since 2011. Around 2.7 million come from Afghanistan, where fighting is ongoing between the US-allied government and the Taliban. And just over one million come from Somalia, where drought, famine, and fighting have displaced large parts of the population. Other countries of origin include Yemen, South Sudan, Iraq, and Eritrea. Another 5.2 million refugees are registered with the United Nations Relief and Works Agency for Palestine Refugees in the Near East. These numbers do not include internally displaced persons, or those who have been forced from their homes but remain in their native country. In Syria alone, that population has reached over six million.

According to **UNICEF**, an estimated one in two hundred children is a refugee. When you include displaced persons or

The ongoing conflict in Darfur has created large refugee communities that are home to millions of people.

migrants, that number increases to one in forty-five children. Although numbers are not available on how many child and adolescent refugees are between the ages of thirteen and eighteen, teenagers are grouped in with the term "child refugee." That has caused controversy, particularly in the United Kingdom where plans to take in child refugees from the **Calais migrant camp** on the French coast led to outcry when some refugees posing as children were found to be over the age of eighteen. It can be difficult to verify the ages of refugees due to a lack of documentation and, in some cases, children not knowing the year they were born. In a small number of cases, programs that are designed to assist children are used by adults posing as teenagers in need of services.

WHERE REFUGEES LIVE

Although the influx of migrants and refugees into Europe has received a great deal of news coverage in recent years, most refugees go to neighboring states rather than more far-off destinations. Turkey, which borders Syria, has the highest number of refugees in the world at 2.5 million. Pakistan, which neighbors Afghanistan, has 1.6 million. Lebanon, which borders both Syria and Israel, hosts 1.1 million refugees—so many that one in five residents of the country are refugees. Iran, Ethiopia, and Jordan also host a large number of refugees from neighboring states.

According to the UNHCR, 55 percent of all global refugees live in Europe or sub-Saharan Africa. In Europe, Italy and Greece are the most common countries of entry into the European Union, while Hungary and Croatia in Eastern Europe also have a high number of migrants and refugees. Germany has taken in the highest number of asylum seekers in Europe, with around 441,900 being registered in 2015. In Africa, Kenya, Uganda, and the Democratic Republic of Congo all host high numbers of refugees, while Chad had the tenth highest refugee population in the world as of 2015, with 369,500. The United States took in 172,700 that same year, with a majority fleeing gang activity and drug cartels in Central America.

TEENAGER RIGHTS UNDER INTERNATIONAL LAW

In 1989, the United Nations General Assembly approved the **Convention of the Rights of the Child**, an agreement that outlines the international rights awarded to people under the age of eighteen. These rights apply to refugees as well as those living in their country of origin, and they speak to the most important features of a healthy life for young people.

The rights outlined by the agreement include the right to education, social security, and family reunification, as well as the right to privacy, information, and respect. Article 22 outlines the additional rights of refugee children:

For young people living in refugee camps, such as these girls in Greece, education and other opportunities are difficult to come by.

1. States Parties shall take appropriate measures to ensure that a child who is seeking refugee status or who is considered a refugee in accordance with applicable international or domestic law and procedures shall, whether unaccompanied or accompanied by his or her parents or by any other person, receive appropriate protection and humanitarian assistance in the enjoyment of applicable rights set forth in the present Convention and in other international human rights or humanitarian instruments to which the said States are Parties.

2. For this purpose, States Parties shall provide, as they consider appropriate, co-operation in any efforts by the United Nations and other competent intergovernmental organizations or non-governmental organizations co-operating with the United Nations to protect and assist such a child and to trace the parents or other members of the family of any refugee child in order to obtain information necessary for reunification with his or her family. In cases where no parents or other members of the family can be found, the child shall be accorded the same protection as any other child permanently or temporarily deprived of his or her family environment for any reason, as set forth in the present Convention.

What this means is that governments are required to help refugee children access resources and make sure they have access to things like education. Those rights include the ones outlined in this particular convention and other international laws to which the country has agreed. For unaccompanied children, states are obligated to try to reunite them with their families, and until doing so have to provide the same protections as they would to any other child without a parent or guardian to look after them. This could include shelter, access to food, and overall safety until the parent or guardian can be contacted. Sadly, many of the rights outlined in the Convention on the Rights of the Child are not met for refugee teenagers, as we'll learn throughout this book. Many young people leave state care or are not honest about their ages to ensure they have the freedom to seek their own families by themselves or to try to work in the country where they are refugees. This leaves many teenagers at risk of exploitation, violence, or other dangers, while they miss out on educational opportunities, access to resources, and their own childhoods.

CHALLENGES TEEN REFUGEES FACE

Refugees under the age of eighteen face unique challenges that demand smart and effective solutions. Many of the issues faced by teenage refugees are due to their lack of access to resources that typical teenagers have, including education, health care, or job training. The financial strain on families can also create dangerous situations in which teens are forced to leave school to support their families or can be exploited by people who want to take advantage of them. In some cases, teens are forced

Girls in refugee camps are particularly vulnerable to exploitation, early marriage, or assault. These girls live in a Somali camp.

into marriages or can be targeted by extremist organizations for recruitment. Many of these teens have also experienced extreme trauma, which requires expert care if these individuals are going to cope in healthy ways. But in many cases, particularly for those living in refugee camps or living without adult supervision in urban spaces, that care and other necessary resources are simply not available.

EDUCATION

For teens around the world, education is the key to ensuring they have access to opportunities. A strong education can provide essential life skills and open the door to further education and career advancement as adults. Yet for teenagers living in refugee camps, education is far from guaranteed. In fact, according to a United Nations report from September 2016, at least 3.7 million school-age kids are not in school. This figure includes 1.95 million teenagers who should be in secondary or high school. While 50 percent of child refugees have access to education, that percentage drops to 22 percent for teenagers. This is a stark drop from the global average of 84 percent. The average amount of time spent **in exile** as refugees is around seventeen years, meaning that education can be difficult to acquire throughout the average educational cycle for those born in refugee camps.

That lack of access to education has dire consequences for these teens' future. Only 1 percent of refugees go on to attend college or university, making it difficult for them to compete for jobs that can bring stability to their adult lives. Education

Many young refugees, like these girls in Pakistan, have to leave school in order to work to support their families.

is also an important way for refugee children to integrate into a society and another way to bring stability to their lives.

There are numerous obstacles that stand between refugee children and access to education. One of the most common is a lack of resources. International organizations struggle to secure supplies, teachers, and space to educate the millions of refugee children in need of classes. Many refugee camps around the world are also in volatile locations. Many parents fear sending their children into the community out of concerns about bullying or harassment. There are also concerns about proper accreditation for programs offered inside refugee camps. While volunteers can teach rudimentary skills, without credentials recognized by the international community, students will struggle to receive higher education or jobs.

Many children living in refugee camps are forced to work to support their families or are unable to secure places in nearby schools due to space limitations and local regulations on enrollment. Although efforts have been made to help ensure students have access to school, organizations like Human Rights Watch argue that they don't go far enough. In Lebanon, for example, two hundred thousand places in public schools have been reserved for Syrian refugees. However, nearly five hundred thousand children need to be placed in classrooms.

TRAUMA

Many of the children and adolescents fleeing war or famine have experienced horrific things or seen those they love killed. As a result, many of them are living with trauma that can make it difficult for them to socialize or learn, as well as causing lasting mental health issues. Depression, anger, isolation, and other effects of trauma can be detrimental to their ability to take part in normal life, and can even lead them to engage in dangerous behavior.

In a 1999 study conducted by a team of researchers in the Netherlands, refugee children who experienced consistent traumatic stressors showed higher rates of physical symptoms than children who did not. The team looked at South Sudanese children living in refugee camps in Uganda and surveyed both Sudanese and Ugandan children. Their study found that Sudanese children who had fled fighting were more likely to have experienced traumatizing life events (such as the loss of their home, lack of food or water, or torture) and daily stressors (such as lack of access to sanitation, concern for family members, or no access to medical care). The effect these experiences had on the children surveyed was significant. They were more likely to experience extreme nervousness, nightmares, aggression, or suicidal thoughts. They also experienced physical effects, including headaches and difficulty sleeping.

While that study was confined to South Sudanese refugees, the lessons apply to teenage refugees across the globe. A 2017 study in the medical journal *The Lancet* found that 33 percent of Syrian refugees between the ages of seven and fourteen living in Germany showed symptoms of post-traumatic stress disorder (PTSD). Trauma experienced by children fleeing war and disaster can include seeing their family members or loved ones killed, becoming ill themselves, and being forced to take part in violence.

PTSD can occur when an individual experiences a dangerous or otherwise highly stressful event, such as those experienced by refugee children and teens. It can manifest in different ways, ranging from short-term symptoms like bad dreams and tension to long-term anxiety, flashbacks, and other psychological issues. People with PTSD can show signs similar to depression, such as loss of interest in previous hobbies or negativity, and some young people stop talking or become unable to be separated from their parents. Teenagers can become aggressive or deal with their difficult emotions by acting out.

PTSD is difficult for everyone who struggles with it, but it poses unique challenges for teen refugees. Those who are unable to communicate effectively can be overlooked and go untreated for their trauma, and those who act out might become caught up in a cycle of punishment that leaves them with few opportunities to deal with their trauma in a healthy way. Treatment for PTSD can include medication, therapy, or other long-term solutions, but few refugees have access to the kind of consistent care that make living with PTSD possible.

But trauma doesn't always end when a refugee finds shelter in a camp or community. A 2014 report by humanitarian organization World Vision found that 86 percent of Syrian refugees between ten and eighteen years old had experienced trauma, including physical violence, in their new communities. Children and adolescents living in refugee camps are at risk of forced labor or sexual violence.

For teenage girls, forced marriage is a very real concern. In 2014, a study found that one in three girls living in refugee camps in Jordan were forced into marriage before turning eighteen. A report published by *The Week* included stories of thirteen- and fourteen-year-old girls being married to twenty-two-year-old and forty-five-year-old men in Lebanese refugee camps. These girls are at risk for physical and emotional abuse, premature pregnancy, and loss of access to education. These marriages, which are often arranged by parents, are carried out for reasons ranging from the family being unable to care for the teenage girl to making a business deal in which a man will pay them money to marry their daughter. In Syrian refugee camps in Jordan, 32 percent of marriages carried out in 2014 involved a girl under the age of eighteen. According to Caroline Anning of Save the Children, "For Syrian refugees who are increasingly in debt and struggling to survive, marrying their daughter off can be seen as the best way to provide for her. With limited job and education opportunities for Syrians, girls often don't see themselves as having much of a future either."

Mona is a fourteen-year-old girl living in Lebanon. Her family fled fighting in Syria, and soon after arriving she married a man much older than her. She told *Mashable:*

> He was twenty-eight years old when I met him, and I was thirteen … I miss school. I would love to go back to school. My dream is to be an airline stewardess. But I know my husband would never allow that. He says that now my role is to take care of our household. I have now simply accepted that this is how my life is going to be.

RADICALIZATION

Children and adolescents in refugee camps are also susceptible to radicalization and recruitment by armed groups and militias. Radicalization is the process by which extremist groups, such as al-Qaeda or ISIS, encourage people to adopt their ideology and

TEEN REFUGEES IN THE NEWS

The refugee crisis has made headlines around the world in recent years, which has played an important role in making it a top priority in countries from Turkey to the United States. But for teen refugees, the media attention tends to swing to two extremes. On one hand, reports of the hardships in camps are common, highlighting the issues they face as they try to carve out normal lives. On the other hand, stereotypes often come into play. Depictions of young adults from countries in the Middle East and Africa often show teen refugees as criminals or dangerous. Reporting like this has a real effect on political policy and the lives of teenage refugees. It also highlights the difficulty in properly communicating complex situations and shows how existing biases can have consequences for teenagers.

An example of this kind of stigmatization can be seen in the United Kingdom, where plans to take in unaccompanied teenagers and children from the Calais migrant camp were disrupted when reports surfaced that some of those applying to enter the country were actually adults. Headlines like "More than two-thirds of so-called 'child refugees' who had their ages assessed were found to be adults" (*The Sun*) flourished, calling into question the trustworthiness of all teenage refugees. Many officials called for more stringent guidelines and assessment, which would prolong the traumatizing experience of living in the refugee camp.

Media coverage of refugees has a real effect on public opinion. Here, people in Idaho protest a rally in support of refugees.

join their forces. Cases of children and teens being targeted for recruitment by militias, terrorist organizations, and other armed groups have been reported from Africa to the Middle East.

There are multiple reasons why refugee camps are seen as key recruiting grounds for armed groups, but according to Rutgers University Professor Simon Reich, one of the main factors is the lack of protection for refugees. Camps are often vulnerable, and according to Reich's research there have been around 1,100 attacks on camps in the last fifty years across Africa. These attacks, and others, create an environment of fear that can make adolescents and teens feel the protection some groups promise is the only way to keep themselves and their loved ones safe.

Another reason teens are drawn into fighting is because some groups are able to offer salaries or other goods, which are difficult to come by in camps otherwise. In Iraq, reports emerged in 2016 that militias were recruiting teenage boys at the Debaga camp by offering around $375 per month, or 447,500 Iraqi dinars. In some situations, the children can be abducted and forced to fight or assist soldiers at camp.

Teens who have been recruited or forced into serving as soldiers or assisting armed groups live through terrible experiences that can have lasting effects on their mental health. Demobilizing them, or taking them off the battlefield and reintegrating them into society, is a difficult task that requires care, time, and patience. Often, they have been forced to commit acts of violence which are then used to manipulate them by leveraging their guilt. Child soldiers are often told they will not be accepted because they are criminals, forcing them to stay with the armed groups. In other cases, child soldiers miss out on months or years of schooling. This issue is worse when they are being recruited from refugee camps where they do not have adequate access to education.

To stop teens from being recruited or abducted by armed groups, experts recommend several actions. Properly monitoring camps and ensuring that armed groups are not present is an important step. So is working to ensure adolescents have a support system or family in the camp. Providing education and training can help combat the sense of hopelessness that contributes to voluntary recruitment. Teaching young people their rights can help them understand how armed groups manipulate those they seek to recruit. One of the most important ways to combat recruitment is properly integrating children into a community so that they feel connected to others and are less easily preyed upon by armed groups. However, this is often a difficult step due to issues like past trauma, lack of education, and the isolation of some camps.

CHAPTER TWO

Teen Refugees in Darfur

M any people think of life as a refugee as temporary, and for some living in a camp is a stopping off point on the way to a new life. But for many, life as a refugee can continue for years—and even decades. **Protracted refugee situations** are, according to the UNHCR, "refugee populations of 25,000 persons or more who have been in exile for five or more years in developing countries." According to a UNHCR report from 2005, at that time around twenty-six different countries had protracted refugee situations around the world. That number does not reflect recent additions like Syria, Iraq, or Yemen.

The number also does not count Darfur, where a **genocide** and civil war that began in 2003 and has since forced millions to flee their homes. Darfur is located in western Sudan,

Opposite: Refugees have been fleeing Darfur since 2003, and many live in makeshift housing in arid conditions.

along the border with Chad. As of 2015, the UNHCR was overseeing 3.7 million refugees in East Africa, a 50 percent increase from 2014. Of those 3.7 million, 3.2 million are considered internally displaced persons because they have not crossed a border, but are still living in refugee camps inside Darfur.

Darfur is home to over two hundred camps for internally displaced persons, or refugees within Darfur's borders. Of the 3.2 million IDPs in Darfur, 1.4 million are under the age of eighteen, according the UNICEF. Many have known no life outside the refugee camps and without the threat of war. These circumstances create challenges that other teenage refugees do not experience. Although refugee camps are designed to be temporary, for many in Darfur they have become something like home. The lack of resources these teens experience contributes to their difficulties. For many teens, childhood ends quickly when living with the danger and scarcity that defines the refugee experience.

DARFUR: THE FIRST GENOCIDE OF THE TWENTY-FIRST CENTURY

Fighting in Darfur began in 2003. That year two rebel groups, the Sudan Liberation Movement and the Justice and Equality Movement (JEM), carried out an attack against the Sudanese government at an air force base in North Darfur. Darfur at that time was a largely underdeveloped area with a majority non-Arab population at odds with the Muslim government in the capital of Khartoum. The government responded to the attack on the air force base by carrying out attacks on civilians in Darfur.

The government has also allegedly empowered the **Janjaweed**, Arab militias made up of populations that have long had conflicts with Darfur's farmers. Drought and civil war created resource scarcity in Darfur, leading to a larger number of attacks and violence between the nomadic Arabs and sedentary non-Arabs. Using the Janjaweed, the government has been accused of killing hundreds of thousands and carrying out a campaign of **ethnic cleansing** against Darfur's non-Arab population. The Janjaweed, who are best known for riding on horse or camelback, use rape as a weapon of war against women and girls and are notorious for their extreme violence against civilians.

Since fighting began in 2003, numerous ceasefires and peace agreements have been signed by the Sudanese government. Despite this, fighting is still ongoing. In fact, the government was accused of using chemical weapons against civilians in 2016. The Janjaweed are a tool of the government in keeping their campaign of genocide underway. Although the international community has alleged that the Janjaweed are directly supported by the Sudanese government, the government denies this. By doing so, Sudan is able to deny responsibility when the Janjaweed continue carrying out attacks despite truces or ceasefires.

The conflict also has a racial element, as non-Arab Darfuris are targeted by the Arab government and Janjaweed. Darfur's non-Arab populations are made up of the Fur, Zaghawa, and Masalit tribes. According to reports, racial epithets are used frequently by the Janjaweed during attacks and less frequently by government forces. Victims of sexual assault have also reported the Janjaweed using racial slurs. It is believed that the government wants to eliminate the non-Arab population in Darfur, amounting to ethnic cleansing.

Young people, including adolescents, were targeted for violence from the earliest days of the fighting. Between 2003 and 2004, just as the conflict was beginning, the Sudanese government was found in violation of the United Nations' **Six Grave Violations Against Children During Armed Conflict.** This UN document is a list of actions considered the most detrimental to the health and safety of young people. The list includes "killing or maiming of children; recruitment or use of child soldiers; rape and other forms of sexual violence against children; abduction of children; attacks against schools or hospitals; and the denial of humanitarian access to children."

LIVING UNDER THREAT

As government forces and the Janjaweed forced Darfuris from their homes and villages, camps began to form across Darfur and into eastern Chad. But while refugee camps are intended to provide shelter for those fleeing ongoing conflict, in many cases they have proven to be far from secure for those who are seeking safety. Attacks on refugee camps in Darfur are common, forcing hundreds and thousands of people at a time to move into different already overcrowded camps elsewhere.

In 2010, Public Radio International profiled Kass, a camp in Darfur where eighty thousand refugees lived. That year, militants rode into the camp and began beating and abducting civilians, demanding the camp pay them blood money for a police officer who had been killed a few days prior. Although the residents of the camp insisted they were not responsible, the

Housing conditions for refugees are often subpar, with large families trying to fit into small, one-room spaces.

attackers abducted one of the camp's leaders and threatened to destroy the camp if their demands were not met. In addition, the attackers burnt a market nearby, destroying around 350 vendor stalls.

In 2013, the Sudanese government created the Rapid Support Forces, which have launched attacks on civilians and refugee populations in the years since with support from militias and the Janjaweed. According to Human Rights Watch, at least two Rapid Support Forces campaigns were carried out against civilians. During these campaigns, forces destroyed food and water sources, assaulted women and girls, and forced the entire population under attack to flee. Those who refused to leave or refused to give up livestock and other resources were killed.

These attacks, which are carried out by the government as well as militia groups, can force thousands of refugees to flee, straining the already limited resources of other camps. For teenagers, this kind of instability can cause further trauma, make them victims of violence or sexual assault, and even prompt them to join armed groups either by choice or by force.

Despite international protection, refugees are vulnerable to attacks by the Janjaweed and other armed militias.

Volatility and danger defines the life of the teenage refugee in Darfur, with little opportunity to establish a sense of normality. Many teens are required to take on responsibilities far beyond their years, bringing their childhoods to a premature end as they help their families and loved ones survive. Between 2005 and 2014, just over twenty thousand refugees from Sudan were resettled elsewhere. Resettlement is one of the best opportunities for full integration in society and a normal life outside of the refugee camps. But for the millions who remain unsettled, including those in Darfur and Chad, the threat of attack by militants, recruitment by armed groups, sexual violence, and lack of resources creates an environment in which it is easy to feel hopeless. Unemployment is high, as is drug use. Today, many hope to seek asylum in Europe, as the camps seem to offer no future.

Idris, who was twenty-seven when he spoke to *Reuters* in 2016, had lived in a refugee camp in Darfur since he was nineteen years old. According to him, immigration to Europe was his "only dream," and would allow him to "start a new life after years of misery."

In the same report, an elder at Zam Zam camp told the interviewer that for young people, there is little that can be done to help them, saying, "The years of their youth fly by while they do nothing; they cannot work or get married and they live like prisoners in these camps."

THE IMPACT OF PROTRACTED REFUGEE SITUATIONS

Protracted refugee situations are unique and challenging phenomena. Refugee efforts—both for protracted events and newly emerging—are often severely underfunded, and refugee camps tend to multiply in countries that are already facing economic strain, such as Ethiopia or Chad. As a result, deciding where to give money is difficult, and the kinds of resources needed to establish safe long-term shelter for refugees are rare. Basic human needs like access to clean water, medical care, safe shelter, and education are often unmet.

Those difficulties are worsened when a refugee situation goes on for a long time with no solutions. As camps become more established, they can become more difficult to move or restructure. Sadly, countries often heavily restrict movement out of the camps for refugees. There are also often restrictions on employment, education, and other activities that makes normal life difficult to engage with for many. Meanwhile, the international community frequently stops paying attention to long-term situations, leading to fewer donations and further difficulty in securing necessary resources and funding.

Life in camps across Darfur and Chad is difficult for teenagers, who are limited in where they can go because of safety concerns and other restrictions. They often have to take on responsibilities that require a lot of time and energy while living with the pain of the war they fled. Sumaya was fifteen when UNICEF interviewed her in 2006, three years after the war began. She and her family lived in Kalma, a camp in South Darfur, with seventy thousand other refugees. For her, life was split between her own studies and helping care for her seven siblings while her parents worked. She helped take care of the housework in their temporary shelter, where she cooked food rations they received twice a month, including beans, oil, salt, and a powdered food mix. Their home often flooded. "During the rainy season, we get wet even when we are inside the house," Sumaya told UNICEF. "There are many holes in the plastic roof, and we sometimes wake up at night all wet and have to sit up for the rest of the night … until the rain stops."

For children and adolescents, these difficulties can have lifelong consequences. A lack of basic needs can impact their mental health and development from an early age, while malnutrition can cause health problems. According to a study published in *The Lancet* in 2011, 75 percent of children in Darfur's camps show signs of post-traumatic stress disorder, and 38 percent show signs of depression.

EDUCATION IN DARFUR

Education can be the key to helping teen refugees secure a stable and fulfilling future. But it can be difficult to guarantee access to schooling for children in refugee camps, particularly

Education in refugee camps is often unofficial, and many classrooms lack adequate resources. Here, Sudanese refugees attend class.

in countries that are facing economic strain as it is. That is true in Darfur and Chad. In Darfur, fighting is ongoing and many camps are not stable due to the threat of violence from militants and the Sudanese government. In Chad, a civil war that raged from 2005 to 2010 has left the country struggling to recover.

Many children have access to primary education in Chad—according to the United Nations, up to 64 percent of children are enrolled in primary schools, but only half of primary schools offer instruction through grade eight. The number of enrolled students drops to 39 percent for secondary education. In classrooms, the teacher-to-student ratio can top fifty to one. Limited resources means it is difficult to furnish classrooms or provide textbooks and materials to the thousands of children in need of education. In some camps, including the large **Abou Shouk** camp with thirty thousand children, there is no secondary school.

Although girls and boys have similar access to education, in Darfur girls are less likely to go to school than boys. Enrollment of girls in some communities is as low as 33 percent. According to ReliefWeb, around 50 percent of girls in West Darfur attend primary school, and only 40 percent of those students go on to secondary school.

There are several reasons for this disparity, including the fact that many teenage girls are expected to help out around the house in ways that boys are not. Girls may be asked to help carry water, gather firewood, or take care of younger siblings, forcing them to leave school. In Abou Shouk, for example, girls are forced to make trips to find resources that can take seven hours or longer total, forcing some to stay away from camp overnight. In other cases, girls are forced to marry while still under the age of eighteen. In some cases, these girls become mothers themselves. Girls who miss out on education for varied circumstances understand the importance of the education they are not receiving.

In order to get water, some teenage girls have to go on a multi-day trip that takes them far from their camps.

"When I'm staying at home and I see other girls going to school, it makes me sad," Amani Suleiman told UNICEF. When she was a teenager, Amani and her siblings were forced to leave school to help their family recover after their livestock were stolen, leaving them with nothing. "In this village, there are more girls at home than at school."

VIOLENCE AGAINST WOMEN

Another threat to teenage girls and others in refugee camps across Darfur is sexual violence. Many women and girls must travel far outside of camps to find water or firewood, leaving them vulnerable to attack by militants or other aggressors. Because of stigmatization or the threat of retaliation, many of these rapes and assaults go unreported. However, organizations like Doctors Without Borders have received reports of up to two hundred cases a month. Experts believe these numbers are actually much lower than the number of assaults that occur. A UNHCR report found that of the reported rapes, one in three victims were under the age of eighteen. According to Amnesty International, cases of assault are more common in refugee camps in Darfur than they are in Chad, although there are numerous reports of guards and other authorities in Chad committing assaults.

Perpetrators of these assaults are both civilians and militants, including government forces and members of the Janjaweed. According to a report by Doctors Without Borders, about one in three of the girls they treated over a six-month period were assaulted by more than one person. These assaults are physically and mentally damaging to the young girls and women who are victimized. Furthermore, pregnancy in camps can be extremely dangerous due to a lack of access to proper medical care. Teenage girls can also find themselves isolated after assaults due to stigma surrounding rape, as reported by Human Rights Watch:

> A sixteen-year-old Fur girl who had been displaced from her village in West Darfur in August 2003 was later raped by three men while collecting firewood outside of the town where she and her family had fled. Following the rape, her family members threw her out of her home and her fiancé broke off their engagement because she was "disgraced." Forced to live alone, she was subjected to further violence, including rape, at the hands of local police who came to her dwelling at night.

Sexual violence is not unique to refugees in Darfur, although it has come to define the public understanding of threats to girls and women. A study published by the National Institutes of Health in 2014 found that around one in five female refugees had been assaulted. The concerns and dangers faced by the women and girls of Darfur are similar to those faced by other refugees, including isolation, lack of medical care, and risk of repeated assault.

There are efforts that have been put in place to protect women and girls in Darfur, particularly in regards to trips outside of camps. Patrols sometimes accompany groups of women and girls beyond the perimeter of the camp as they gather firewood and other resources. Yet these patrols might not always take place when women need to leave camp. Other efforts include

Young women collect firewood in Darfur. These kinds of chores take them away from school and expose them to danger.

introducing alternative fuels sources and methods of cooking. Ultimately, however, the only way to truly protect girls from assault is to provide them with stable and secure homes in communities that are not threatened with ongoing violence.

MILITIAS

As in other refugee situations, children and adolescents are targeted by armed groups for recruitment. Recruitment has been carried out by rebel groups (including the Justice and Equality Movement) and government-aligned forces. According to the United Nations, in 2007 around seven thousand to ten thousand children living in refugee camps had been forced to join armed groups. Another study the next year found that six thousand child soldiers were being used, including children as young as eleven. Since then, rebel groups have begun demobilizing child soldiers. In 2010, JEM signed a deal to halt recruitment of soldiers under eighteen years old, but use of child soldiers continues in other groups and government forces.

A DAY IN THE LIFE

Teenage life in refugee camps in Darfur and Chad looks very little like the average teenage experience in other parts of the world. Most young people are forced to take on the responsibilities of adulthood quickly, which leaves little time for friends or fun. Meeting basic needs for themselves and their families takes up the bulk of their time and dominates the days of the average young person.

Days start early at refugee camps, and cooking requires a lot of effort. Caring for the wood-fire stoves and rationing food aid between the many people in any given family means that mornings are already packed with important jobs for teenagers who help preparing meals.

Very few teenagers in Darfur or Chad attend school, including only 20 percent of girls. Boys who don't go to school might have a job in the camp or in nearby villages. With little opportunity available, jobs are often dangerous and low paying. Those who do go to school often have to make long journeys to get to class, which takes up most of their non-school hours. The journey can be dangerous, as militants and armed groups often kidnap or attack young people who have left camp.

Day-to-day life for teenage girls in Darfur refugee camps is often devoted to helping meet the needs of their families. Many young girls instead help take care of their younger siblings, cook, or otherwise take care of the home. Gathering firewood, water, food, and other resources can take hours—sometimes over seven hours round trip. Some young girls are forced to spend the night far from camp, where they are vulnerable to attack.

At the end of the day, many teenagers are unable to leave their tents or homes because of security concerns. International organizations have worked to ensure refugee housing has electricity, but many do not. This means that it is hard for students to do their homework at night. Teens often have no privacy due to cramped housing they share with their families. In the morning, the cycle of chores begins again.

These young men are former child soldiers. Young refugees are sometimes recruited by extremist groups to be soldiers.

In 2015, Human Rights Watch conducted extensive interviews with former child soldiers in Darfur, including a nineteen-year-old named Ibrahim. He was recruited into the Rapid Support Forces when he was seventeen and took part in an attack shortly thereafter. During the attack, he was ordered to abuse women, destroy property, and kill civilians, including a young woman.

"I am deeply sorry. But you must understand that this was not my endeavor, I was under the command of men with no mercy. I wish I could turn back the time," he told interviewers when asked if he had anything he wanted to say to the family of his victims.

But boys aren't the only ones who are targeted by armed groups. Girls are also victims. In some cases they are recruited to fight, but more often they are abducted, particularly by the

Janjaweed. These girls and young women are repeatedly abused, forced to carry children, and in some cases injured so severely that they may never recover. In other cases, when they attempt to escape they are killed.

Ibrahim and others like him are both victims and perpetrators, a difficult combination of identities that often creates long lasting trauma due to grief, guilt, and other mental health issues. Girls who are abducted also face long-term consequences, including isolation and rejection by their families or the burden of caring for children. Teenagers who become involved with these armed groups, as is true around the world, miss out on important access to education, familial connections, and often food and water. They are traumatized again and again, and their rehabilitation takes time and patience as they recover from the actions they witnessed, took part in, and suffered.

ECONOMIC SITUATIONS OF HOST COUNTRIES

The economic circumstances of countries that host camps have a large impact on the lives of refugees, who often rely on host countries to provide basic resources and funding alongside humanitarian organizations. Wealthier countries, which tend to take in fewer refugees than impoverished states, are also better equipped to offer refugees jobs, education, and other opportunities that better position them to achieve stability.

The economy in Darfur prior to the conflict starting in 2003 was largely agricultural. A long drought had created a strain on farmers even before violence uprooted millions. Those skills, which are now not being passed down to younger generations, are of little help in refugee camps with little room to plant crops. With violence ongoing, the Darfur economy is unlikely to rebound in a way that could guarantee a return to stable farming or provide livelihoods for the millions who have fled their homes. The economy in Chad is similarly strained, due to civil conflict and high unemployment. Although some refugees have been able to work in markets or find jobs with organizations that work in refugee camps, such as educational groups, young people often have to find jobs in mines or other hard

This map of Sudan shows how close Darfur (in the country's left hand corner) is to neighboring Chad. Refugees from Darfur tax Chad's already strained economy.

labor positions in neighboring countries. These young people are under threat of exploitation by employers who pay low wages for dangerous work. Yet teens often seek these jobs in order to help support their families or save up money to pay traffickers to get them to Europe.

CHAPTER THREE

Teen Refugees in Jordan

Some of the crises that have produced the highest number of refugees since 2010 have taken place in the Middle East. From the Syrian Civil War to ongoing conflict in Iraq to the Yemeni Civil War, conflicts in the region have forced millions to flee their homes and seek shelter in neighboring states. Many have found their way to Jordan, a country with a long history of accepting refugees. Jordan is bordered by Israel, Palestine, Syria, Iraq, and Saudi Arabia, and it has a small coast that connects it to Egypt and the Horn of Africa via the Gulf of Aqaba. Since 1948, when a large influx of Palestinian refugees settled in, Jordan has been one of the region's—and the world's—primary host countries for Middle Eastern and African refugees. Today the county hosts millions of Palestinians and hundreds of thousands of Syrians, Iraqis, Somalis, Yemenis, and Sudanese.

Opposite: Zaatari is Jordan's largest refugee camp. Refugees have opened businesses to serve those living there.

Unlike in Darfur, refugees in Jordan live in both camps and cities. According to the World Bank, refugees make up around 40 percent of Jordan's population, with Syrians accounting for about one-tenth. **Zaatari**, a refugee camp that was established in 2012 for Syrian refugees, is home to around eighty thousand people. Palestinians, many of whom have lived in Jordan for generations, often hold Jordanian nationality while maintaining refugee status. An estimated 140,000 Palestinians registered with the UNHCR do not have Jordanian nationality.

For teenage refugees, Jordan offers a level of stability that other refugee host countries often don't. Although there are still difficulties, including limited access to food in some camps and a lack of job opportunities, teens are able to receive education at steadier levels, engage with the economy in their own refugee camps or in cities, and otherwise live like kids. As we'll see, some teenagers are even advocating for their own communities and helping make life better for their fellow refugees. But dangers, including crime and gender-based violence, are still an ever-present threat for those who live in Jordanian refugee populations.

WHERE REFUGEES IN JORDAN ARE FROM

In many host countries, such as Turkey or Lebanon, refugee populations are relatively new. The country has not had experience hosting and providing for the needs of refugee populations. As a result, the learning curve can cause problems given the immediacy of refugee needs. But Jordan has been hosting refugees since 1948, and that experience can be seen in how they manage large influxes of refugee populations, including the one they experienced after the Syrian Civil War began in 2011. The country, which has one of the highest refugee populations in the world, is a melting pot of refugees from around the Middle East and the Horn of Africa, all of whom have fled conflict in the past seven decades.

PALESTINE

Jordan has seen large numbers of Palestinian refugees entering the country multiple times since 1948. The refugee population was established in Jordan, as well as Lebanon and Syria, following the 1948 Palestine War. This war pitted Arab Palestinians against British and Israeli forces shortly before the declaration of the State of Israel. More fled during the Six Days War, between Israel and several Arab states, in 1967. Other outbreaks of fighting between Israel and the Palestinian Territories have forced others to flee into Jordan as well. Today, most Palestinians have citizenship in Jordan. Many have been living in the country for multiple generations.

There are approximately 2,117,361 registered Palestinian refugees in Jordan as of 2015, according to the United Nations Relief and Works Agency for Palestinian Refugees in the Near East (UNRWA). The UNRWA oversees ten official refugee camps for Palestinians, which house around 370,000 people, or 18 percent of the Palestinian population in Jordan. The agency also manages 174 schools, 23 clinics, and a microfinance loan program that has awarded over $83 million to help Palestinians establish businesses.

JORDAN'S ECONOMY

Jordan has a small economy compared to other Middle Eastern states, and the nation has limited access to natural resources like oil and water. Therefore, the country relies on foreign aid and struggles with high poverty and unemployment. This economic situation has created issues for refugees both inside camps and outside of them, in part due to the lack of available jobs and homes for those who are not in UNHCR camps. Jordan's budget is also strained, making it hard for the country to fund refugee resources. The country has, however, worked to make sure that Syrian refugees are not forgotten. The government announced plans to introduce thousands of jobs for Syrians. According to Oxfam, the country spends around $870 million per year to help Syrian refugees, a total that amounts to around 5,622 percent of a traditional donor's "fair share" according to the organization's metrics.

This kind of aid, however, has come at a political cost. The country was already struggling economically. The influx of refugees has been used as a scapegoat for those looking to place blame. Many Jordanians feel that refugees are being given too much when there is already too little for citizens, although studies do not support claims that refugees are taking jobs Jordanians

Like we saw in the case of Chad in the previous chapter, Jordan's economy faces strain from hosting refugees.

could otherwise fill. It is unclear whether Jordan will be able to afford to remain as welcoming to refugees as the country has been. It is even more unclear what country could fill that vacuum if Jordan is unable to care for those in need.

IRAQ

There are approximately 61,405 Iraqi refugees living in Jordan and registered with the UNHCR as of 2017. However, it is believed that the number is much higher when counting those who live in cities rather than refugee camps. Refugees began arriving in Jordan following the 1991 Gulf War, when the United States targeted Saddam Hussein's government. Another influx of Iraqi refugees came to Jordan following the 2003 invasion of Iraq by United States coalition forces.

There were few restrictions on movement for Iraqis entering Jordan at that time, making it easy for refugees to settle into urban spaces. Since then, many Iraqis have struggled to integrate fully, and unemployment rates are high. Only an estimated 30

Early marriage is a widespread problem among refugee populations in Jordan. Girls, like the young woman pictured, often lose their chance at an education when they marry young.

percent of Iraqi men are working in Jordan. The percentage drops to around 14 percent for women. This is due to the lack of legal documentation many have, and it has forced many highly skilled refugees—including doctors—to take positions that do not reflect their knowledge and experience or to work for low wages.

YEMEN

Today there are an estimated 2,000 Yemeni refugees in Jordan, although around 1,600 are registered with UNHCR. Yemen fell into civil war in 2015, when rebels began clashing with government forces. Fighting intensified when Saudi Arabia began supporting the government that year. Although the fighting has displaced over two million civilians, many of them have been displaced internally. The vast majority of refugees have gone to Djibouti or Saudi Arabia, while those who have gone to Jordan for medical treatment or other needs often want to return to Yemen rather than establish themselves as refugees.

SOMALIA AND SUDAN

Syrian, Palestinian, and Iraqi refugees often receive the most media attention, but they are not the only refugees present in Jordan. The country also has around four thousand refugees from other countries, predominantly Somalia and Sudan. Most are fleeing fighting or famine but do not qualify for Jordan's priority programs designed to help those in immediate need. Therefore, some have to wait for over a year as their requests for asylum are processed and another month or two before they are formally registered as refugees with UNHCR. Many spend a long amount of time in limbo, without access to resources other than a one-time payment through the UNHCR for which they must apply and be approved. "There is security in Jordan, but nothing else," one Sudanese refugee told the Carnegie Endowment for International Peace.

SYRIA

Since the start of the Syrian Civil War in 2011, millions of Syrians have fled to Turkey, Lebanon, Jordan, and other countries. According to the United Nations, there are an estimated 656,170 registered Syrian refugees in Jordan as of February 2017. Over half of the refugees in Jordan are under the age of seventeen, and many have serious medical or mental health issues in need of addressing.

As of late 2016, tens of thousands were stranded in **"the berm,"** a stretch of desert between Jordan and Syria. The estimated 85,000 are living in a camp called Rukban, which technically lies on Syrian soil, in part due to concerns over possible infiltration by ISIS. Those fears seemed to be confirmed in early 2017 when a car bomb was detonated in the camp and ISIS issued warnings about possible attacks in the future. Of the thousands living in Rukban and "the berm," the UN claims that the vast majority are women and children under the age of eighteen.

TEENAGE LIFE IN REFUGEE CAMPS

The Zaatari refugee camp is a large, sprawling city of tents and low structures. Although the homes and structures are low to the ground and were set up quickly, the camp—which is home to around eighty thousand Syrians and is Jordan's fourth-largest city—features businesses, cafes, schools, clinics, and other staples you would expect in a community that size.

But life in camps like Zaatari is still difficult for kids. Around ninety thousand are not in school, and many have to work to help support their families. Ahmed, who was thirteen years old when he spoke to UNICEF in 2015, left school at age twelve when his family fled Syria. His father was unable to come with them, so Ahmed and his brother had to begin working when they arrived in Zaatari to help support their family. Stories like Ahmed's are common; a study found that around 13 percent of children between the ages of seven and seventeen in Zaatari held jobs.

Efforts have been made to ensure these teens get education. Ahmed and others are welcome to take classes at **drop-in centers**,

Zaatari refugee camp is Jordan's fourth largest city.

which allow flexible schedules so that teens who need to work are able to do so without sacrificing their education. These centers are in addition to schools serving just refugees and almost one hundred public schools that offer "double shifts" during the day and at night around the country. **Adolescent-Friendly Spaces**, or AFS, have also been set up around camps to provide a safe space for young people to learn skills, engage in crafts, and work through trauma they experienced while socializing with their peers.

Muzon, a Syrian girl who fled her country in 2013 and came to live in Zaatari, was forced to leave school to go to Jordan. But Muzon understood that education was the key to a bright future. "I didn't need them to tell me that education was important," the seventeen-year-old told UNHCR in 2015. "I always just felt it ... Education is everything in life."

In many refugee situations, teens have few opportunities to take their lives into their own hands. They are bound by limited resources and the need to work, making it hard to find time to advance causes they believe in. But Muzon decided that she wanted to do something to help fellow Syrian girls and women by helping ensure they have access to education. She campaigns on behalf of young girls and advocates for better access to education and opportunity. "When I hear of people not letting their daughters go to school or marrying them off early, it makes me angry," she said. "Education is the armor that will protect you in life. If you get married before finishing your education, you won't be able to solve your own problems or educate your own children."

As Muzon has seen, not all girls are able to take full advantage of the educational opportunities offered by Jordan and UNHCR, as well as other organizations. In Zaatari, early marriage is common, with one in three registered marriages involving a girl under the age of eighteen. These marriages, which are undertaken for reasons including financial support for the girls' families or in order to provide a better life for the girls, can be abusive and often force the young girls to leave school to care for their home or their own children.

Syrian girls attend a clinic in Ramtha, Jordan.

TEENAGE LIFE IN CITIES

The vast majority of refugees in Jordan live in cities rather than camps. This presents unique challenges and opportunities. On one hand, city life allows young people to better integrate with Jordanian society. On the other hand, these refugees are cut off from access to resources offered by organizations like the UNHCR at refugee camps. For teenagers, that can mean that it's a challenge to access education, food, medical care, and other necessary services.

Part of the difficulty facing refugees living outside of camps in Jordan is that the country does not offer a legal status for refugees. According to the Law Library of Congress, refugees are often referred to as "'visitors,' 'irregular guests,' 'Arab brothers,' or simply 'guests.'" Therefore, they do not have a legal standing that affords them special access to necessary services. The Jordanian government has also not received as much foreign assistance as it needs to help shoulder the burden of public services that the huge growth in population has created. These burdens include the influx of students entering schools and the demands of treating refugees' medical and mental health concerns.

Life for teenage refugees in Jordanian communities is difficult to track because these teens are not monitored or served the

Despite international efforts, many young people in refugee camps in Jordan struggle to gain access to necessary resources.

way those in camps are. The Jordanian government allows all children access to public education and limited medical care via public subsidies. But most families struggle to make ends meet due to restrictions on employment for non-citizens, forcing some young people to take jobs rather than pursue their education. These jobs can be exploitative and dangerous because they are often informal and unregulated.

For those who are able to attain education, however, studies show that adolescents living outside of camps are more likely to go on to higher education, particularly among Palestinians. Literacy rates are also higher among those who live outside of camps, and girls outperform boys when it comes to education. Yet the educational system has been put under extreme strain as the refugee population has grown. Jordan has called on the international community to help them sustain refugees.

Teenagers in communities also face discrimination. In recent years, the strain on services and the economy has led to public opinion largely turning against refugees. Frustrations are sometimes taken out on young people. A Syrian refugee named Ibrahim told the *Middle East Monitor* that he had to take his teenage children out of school after they were treated badly by teachers. This kind of bullying can create a sense of isolation for teens, giving them few social outlets and no connection to the communities in which they might spend years of their lives.

A DAY IN THE LIFE

Life is very different in Jordan than it was in Syria before the civil war began there in 2011. Many teenagers have reported that while their life in Syria was straightforward and easy, living in a refugee camp is much more difficult. The average refugee teenager living in Zaatari refugee camp starts their day as early as 6:00 a.m. Most young people help take care of their family, and one of the first things that needs to be done is getting bread for the day. The wait in line can take up to half an hour. Chores and helping with housework is an important part of many teenagers' routines, whether it's helping to cook or care for siblings. Most families live in small, crowded spaces, with as many as thirteen in one tent.

Many teenagers in refugee camps and in cities have to take jobs to help support their families. These jobs can require them to work long hours—sometimes up to twelve-hour days. Some of those kids also find time to go to classes at a school or at a center where they can take classes. These centers are an important way for kids who aren't able to go to school full time to continue learning skills and socializing. Other teenagers are able to go to school during the day. Many teenagers are able to make friends and find community through schools and classes, which is an important part of building a life while living in the camp. Classes in photography and videography have flourished in Jordanian refugee camps, giving kids an important and fun outlet to channel their time and energy and to share their lives with the outside world.

Some young girls are unable to go to school because their parents choose to arrange marriages for them instead, which can be seen as a better way to secure a future for them. These girls often have to stay home during the day. Many say that it makes them sad to watch other kids their age going to school and classes. Some of these girls have children of their own to take care of.

Days are long in refugee camps, and chores often continue into the night as young people help care for their families. Boys and girls are expected to help out with chores, which can include getting rations and water or cleaning among other tasks. In addition to helping out their families, teenagers also have to find time for homework. Many don't get to go to bed until late in the night, and they have to wake up again early the next day to start their routine over again.

CHAPTER FOUR

Teen Refugees in Greece

While Jordan has hosted refugees for generations and Darfur has experienced a protracted refugee situation, Greece has only experienced an influx of refugees in the past decade. Since 2015, the International Rescue Committee estimates that 1.3 million people have traveled to Greece en route to Europe, and over 65,000 are being housed in some fifty camps on Greek islands and mainland. With no long-term structures or resources, many of these refugees—half of whom are women and children—have had to struggle through cold winters, blistering summers, and a total lack of normality.

A DANGEROUS CROSSING

Refugees come to Greece from countries such as Syria, Iran, and Libya. Many pass through Turkey, another country with a high number of refugees, before being smuggled across the Mediterranean by guides. This can be expensive and dangerous,

Opposite: More than one million people, including hundreds of thousands of teens and children, have fled to Greece since 2015.

costing families years of savings just to send one or two family members, let alone their entire family.

Greece has islands that are very close to the coast of Turkey, making it a primary destination for refugees seeking access to the European Union. Four islands have seen a massive influx of refugees. Lesbos has around 5,200 refugees. Chios has around 3,300. And Samos and Kos both have around 1,300. Yet even getting that far is dangerous, and many refugees have died on the journey.

Mitra was sixteen years old when he decided to leave his native Afghanistan in 2013. His father had been working for the military when he was killed by members of the Taliban. Fearing danger, he chose to leave his family and make the journey to Europe. "My cousin arranged everything," Mitra told Doctors Without Borders after arriving in Greece. "I went to Kandahar and from there to Pakistan—[the city of] Quetta. It took me three days to reach Iran. I went to Tehran and from there to Urmia, near the border. I stayed there for three days in a house with 15 more people. Then we left for the mountains."

Mitra joined up with a group that was getting to Greece via a river, the Evros River, that runs between Turkey and Greece. He and the twenty-four others who were traveling with the group were given plastic inflatable boats by **smugglers**. Two of the boats, carrying eight people total, capsized, and one person died while trying to swim to shore. When Mitra and the others made it to Greece, it was already four in the morning, and they were disoriented. They made it to a village, where someone called the police. "They took us to a big **detention center**. When I was asked about my age, I said that I was sixteen years

The international migrant and refugee crisis has left millions without homes, including many living in camps in Greece.

old and the interpreter wrote nineteen. The following day I was released and I went to Athens," Mitra said.

Mitra was fortunate. For those crossing the Mediterranean, the trip often proves deadly. The boats Mitra and his group were given are common. Smugglers give refugees flimsy boats and life vests full of sawdust and other materials that prove useless if disaster strikes. Although it is impossible to know how many have died due to capsized boats, experts believe that in 2016 around five thousand people died making the crossing. Sunny, a seventeen-year-old from Pakistan, told *VICE* about the long trip he made through Greece to Austria after two of his friends were kidnapped by terrorists:

I traveled through Iran, Turkey, Greece, Macedonia, Croatia, Serbia, and Austria. My father is retired from the military; he gave me €6,000 [$6,800] for my journey. I traveled mainly by paying people to take me in their cars. Often there were many, many people squeezed in—ten in the back seat and five in the front. To get to Greece I got in a three-by-nine-foot boat. I was half in the water and half in the boat. When we landed, the army directed us to a camp, and we were sent first to Germany and then on to Sicily.

Many are trying to get to Germany or the United Kingdom but become entangled in a complex bureaucracy that has left thousands stranded. Refugees are held in detention centers or camps that do not properly keep them safe from the cold—all are meant to be temporary measures but people live there for months and months. Meanwhile, refugees do not have access to formal employment and have limited food, clothing, and other resources. Until 2016, there were no plans in place to ensure school-age refugees are able to attend classes. Medical care is also scarce despite best efforts by international organizations.

In countries in northern and central Europe, the influx of refugees has created political crises. Right-wing parties in France, the UK, Norway, and more have stoked fears about the high number of refugees from the Middle East and elsewhere to support harsher restrictions on immigration. As a result, countries like Greece and Italy where refugees are able to get ashore without papers are faced with the daunting and difficult task of processing claims for asylum, assisting in resettlement,

Refugees traveling to Greece use dangerous sea routes, often on boats that are overcrowded or otherwise hazardous.

and providing for the populations while they are waiting for a more permanent solution.

An agreement between Greece and Turkey in late 2016 was meant to help ease the strain on the country, returning some refugees and migrants to Turkey while the European Union began resettling refugees who were in Turkey. This was meant to end the illegal flow of people across the border, but the result was an effective freeze on the refugees currently waiting for accommodation in Greece.

UNACCOMPANIED TEENAGERS

Among the thousands of refugees in Greece are numerous unaccompanied minors. In the first seven months of 2016, Greece registered around 3,300 unaccompanied minors, but the number could be higher. As of 2016, an estimated 10,000 refugees under the age of eighteen had simply gone "missing," living on their own and impossible to provide services to. Young people often lie about their age to be released into their own care, and many refugees do not register with authorities at all out of fear of being sent back. Unaccompanied children have been reportedly kept in detention with adults, without access to medical treatment and other resources that are guaranteed to them under international and European Union law. Rebecca Riddell wrote for Human Rights Watch about a young boy named Wasim, whom she met in a detention center in Greece:

> Wasim is a sixteen-year-old Kurdish boy who fled Mosul, Iraq, seeking a safe haven after Islamic State (IS) executed his father. Unfortunately for Wasim, he

ended up stuck in a tiny, dirty cell in a small-town police station in northwest Greece. When I met Wasim, he had been locked up around the clock for a month, without access to interpreters, psychological care, or even games or books to occupy his mind.

Young people can end up alone in Greece for many reasons. One of the most common is that a family will send their children to safety even though they cannot afford to send an adult with them. Marina Spyridaki is a psychologist working with Doctors Without Borders. In 2015, she shared her observations on the island of Kos, including meeting a young boy who was sent away by his family for his own safety:

There was a fourteen-year-old Syrian boy who arrived here on his own. A woman working at the port saw him crying day after day and asked us to help him. He was desperate to go back to Turkey, where his mother was. He felt he just couldn't survive without her. But it had been the family's decision for him to leave, and it wasn't possible for him to go back.

Life for refugees in Greece is largely unstructured. Schools were only established in October 2016, with a limited number of children being granted access. High school age students were not allowed to begin classes when other students did because secondary schools claimed that without proof the students finished primary school, they could not be admitted.

The lack of resources for teenagers is a huge problem in Greece. Many young people do not speak or read Greek,

Refugee camps in Greece were set up quickly as temporary shelter, but many refugees have been living there for months.

which makes it difficult for them to advocate for themselves without a translator. The inability to communicate means they cannot truly control their own case and ensure that their needs are being met, relying instead on the availability of interpreters and resources. Many young people choose to leave the camps and live in cities, where they could become homeless. Hundreds live in squats, or abandoned buildings where numerous refugees live together and some volunteers are able to provide limited services.

Young people often come to Greece in hopes of a better future, something their families also hope they are able to find. Others want to establish themselves so that they can bring their families to Europe. But most often they do not find the opportunities they had hoped for. Seventeen-year-old Karim told the *Guardian* that he hoped to work in a supermarket owned by his uncle in Germany when his family sent him to Europe from Afghanistan. Instead, he has been forced to sell drugs to make ends meet in Athens, the capital of Greece.

Karim's story is common. Teenagers who find themselves on the streets of Athens or other cities are more and more frequently turning to crime in attempts to raise funds for the trip to central Europe. Some, such as two teenage boys named Alsaleh and Jasim, are forced to assist smugglers in transporting people across the border. For Alsaleh and Jasim, their role ended when they were arrested on charges of trafficking.

Some young people are exploited by gangs or people looking for cheap labor. There are reports of young boys being offered a day's work, only to be forced to work for weeks unpaid. In other cases, teenage boys are forced into prostitution either by circumstances or by gang leaders.

Whether living on the streets or in detention centers, many teenagers feel they are not living up to their full potential or being given the freedom they thought they would find in Europe. They are also grappling with the trauma they experienced in their home countries, during the process of fleeing, and since arriving in Greece. Many also have family left behind, who they worry about and miss immensely. "Sometimes I feel so angry that I can't breathe, and then I fall unconscious," seventeen-year-old Abouni told the *Guardian*. "I have family in Syria under the bombs, and when I talk to my little sister on the phone, she asks if she'll ever see me again. I'm stuck here in this jail."

Teenagers sometimes lie about their age or circumstances to avoid being detained, opting to make it on their own in cities like Athens.

Hopelessness is the dominant feeling among many teenage refugees living in Greece. "The worst thing is I am in Greece for nothing," Hassan, a fifteen-year-old living in an abandoned school in Athens with other refugees, told the *Guardian*. "I am wasting my life here, not going to school—waiting for nothing. At home I felt I was alive. I did what I wanted. I studied. I lived my life. I played football."

GIRLS AT RISK

Most of the available information about adolescent refugees in Greece focuses on the plight of teenage boys. This is for a simple reason: unaccompanied minors are often boys, because parents feel it is safer for them to travel alone. But teenage girls are also living through the difficulties of life in Greece, and they face very real threats.

Women told Amnesty International that they felt largely unsafe in refugee spaces in Greece, where they were sometimes forced to use the same facilities as men. Those who had to pay smugglers to make the crossing to Greece or elsewhere in Europe reported being threatened with sexual assault on several occasions. Nahla, a twenty-year-old, had to rely on a male cousin to step in when a smuggler began harassing and touching her.

For those who reach Greece and other settlements, the fear does not go away. The lack of space creates situations where men and women have to sleep close together, which for some is a violation of cultural norms. Many women and girls are unable to sleep for fear of being attacked or assaulted by men. One of them, Reem, is traveling with a fifteen-year-old female cousin whom she is trying to protect, telling Amnesty International:

I never got the chance to sleep in settlements. I was too scared that anyone would touch me. The tents were all mixed and I witnessed violence ... I felt safer in movements, especially on the bus, the only place I could shut my eyes and sleep. In the camps we are so prone to being touched, and women can't really complain and they don't want to cause issues to disrupt their trip.

Some teenage girls have experienced abuse at the hands of authorities, including police and other guards. Maryam is sixteen and came to Greece from Syria. She told Amnesty International that she was beaten by police and refused medical attention:

People started screaming and shouting, so the police attacked us and was hitting everyone with sticks. They hit me on my arm with a stick. They even hit younger kids. They hit everyone even on the head. I got dizzy and I fell, people were stepping on me. I was crying and was separated from my mother. They called my name and I was with my mother. I showed them my arm and a police officer saw my arm and laughed. I asked for a doctor, they asked me and my mother to leave.

COMMUNITY COMING TOGETHER

Although the Greek government has struggled to ensure that refugees have access to necessary services, volunteers from around the world have come together to make life better for the most vulnerable among them. Help Refugees is a network of volunteers who work in Athens, providing meals and classes at their own facility and serving meals and handing out goods where they can. For the hundreds who live in squats, or illegal abandoned buildings, Help Refugees has worked to pay for food and get access to hot water, a crucial step in guaranteeing sanitation for those living there. Volunteers also work on the beaches and ports where refugees tend to land, providing translation, food, clothing, and other services as they can. Greeks themselves are also coming together to help refugees by providing clothing, food, diapers, and other goods to those in need, as well as pressuring the government to do more for refugees.

For teenagers, services like language classes and meal services can be life changing. Help Refugees also offers safe spaces, where teens are able to sleep or just spend time without fear of gangs or other threats. In the vacuum created by the lack of programs for teenagers, organizations like Help Refugees can make a big difference in the lives of teenage refugees living in Greece.

THE GLOBAL IMPACT OF REFUGEES AND MIGRANTS IN GREECE

Greece has become the epicenter of a world-changing migrant and refugee crisis. For the West, the impact of the refugee crisis can be seen in the public perception and opinion of immigration. In Europe, people tend to blame immigrants—and refugees with them—for crime and economic strain. In Greece and Italy, where many refugees land after crossing the Mediterranean, 70 percent and 60 percent of respondents see immigrants as a burden who take jobs and use social benefits. In Germany, a country that has taken in a high number of refugees for resettlement, 40 percent believe immigrants are responsible for more crimes than other groups. What's more, anti-immigration parties in Europe are seeing political gains from France to the United Kingdom to Denmark. Other countries, like Austria and Hungary, have tightened their border restrictions to ensure that refugees aren't able to get past without registering. Islamophobia has been cited as one reason why there is a great deal of pushback against assisting refugees, as most refugees are coming from Middle Eastern countries. Attacks by ISIS in Europe have been pointed to as justification of anti-immigration measures, although refugees have been found to pose no threat to host communities.

Greece, shown here in white, is sometimes called the gateway to Europe.

Despite these polls, there are many in Europe who want to assist refugees and make sure they are safe. The United Kingdom has worked to offer resettlement to unaccompanied teenagers, and volunteers from across Europe have traveled to high impact areas to lend their support.

CHAPTER FIVE

Looking Ahead

Widespread mass migration is changing our world from day to day. Refugees not only bring an influx of new skills, knowledge, perspective, and experiences to their host communities; they are also changing the demographics of countries around the world. But often host countries are ill-equipped to handle the large population increases that come with refugees, all of whom have unique and critical needs that require resources many countries simply do not have. Due to shortages of resources, the potential of refugees is put on hold or erased completely as they struggle to survive.

For teenage refugees, it can be difficult to know what the future might hold. Some refugees who have fled may be able to return to their homes during their lifetimes, but others could live the rest of their lives away from their country of origin. If so, they will join the many who have made a future for themselves in new countries under unexpected circumstances.

Opposite: Syrian refugees protest being barred from boarding trains in Budapest in 2015. They were stuck at the train station for two days.

For internally displaced persons, they could live in a new part of their country for years before returning to a radically changed version of the home they once knew.

In the meantime, the needs of refugees are immediate and important but difficult to meet. Young people need access to medical care and help processing the trauma they have experienced, along with basic needs like food, water, and shelter. They also need access to education, something the majority of teenage refugees do not have. Without these resources, young people will have difficulty adjusting to life as adults and fully realizing their potential.

While organizations and individuals are doing their best to help these vulnerable populations, there is still much that needs to take place before teenage refugees are fully cared for. Key steps for making sure their needs are met start with identifying the population, which can be difficult when many teens, particularly in Greece and elsewhere in Europe, see benefits in staying below the radar of the authorities.

Refugees will be one of the driving forces of change in coming years and decades, and that is particularly true for teenagers who are coming of age under these extraordinary circumstances. Understanding how their needs can be met in a timely, beneficial way is crucial to giving these young people the opportunities they deserve and want.

HOW REFUGEES ARE CHANGING THE WORLD

Refugees and their children have always made important contributions to society. From Albert Einstein to Freddie Mercury to Steve Jobs, being granted asylum and being allowed to resettle has made it possible for people to change the way we see science, the arts, and technology, among other things. But the number of people on the move around the world today is nearly unprecedented, and the effect it can have on mankind remains to be seen.

It can be difficult to understand what it means to have 65.3 million people uprooted from their homes and living as

Protests in support of refugee rights have taken place around the world, highlighting the global concern for refugee well-being.

refugees. To get a sense of how many people that is, consider this: if all refugees were considered their own country, it would be the twenty-fourth largest on the globe with more people than Britain.

The impact this widespread displacement is having on our world is both seen and unseen. Visuals of people making their way across the Mediterranean, living in tent cities, or crowding islands that were once vacation destinations are an immediately recognizable reminder of what the term "refugee crisis" means. But the lasting impact of this kind of migration is harder to see, and can take decades to truly be understood.

Economically, refugees could reshape the countries in which they are currently living, if allowed to fully participate in the workforce. Many refugees are highly skilled—doctors, lawyers, teachers, and others are among those fleeing hardship. But they often find that their credentials do not transfer to other countries, and they find themselves working low pay jobs to make ends meet. If countries streamlined efforts to allow these trained professionals to work in their fields of expertise, entire professions could be reformed with their skills and knowledge. In addition, studies have found that immigrants claim less in benefits and services than they contribute in taxes, meaning that letting refugees participate in the economy could lead to growth for communities hosting them.

In many countries, refugees are encountering already strained systems, and young people are often missing out on opportunities. Most refugees are currently in low-income countries, where high unemployment and lacking public resources were issues before refugees began arriving in large numbers. This can have an immediate impact on the kinds of resources available to refugees. In countries like Chad, poor access to food and water are issues for the population at large and particularly for refugees. In Lebanon, the education system was under strain before millions of refugees arrived. Now, the country is unable to keep up with the needs of young people, particularly teenagers.

Politically, refugees are largely without power today. They are unable to vote in their host communities, have no formal representation on the world stage, and are often without agency in their countries of origin. Yet in many countries, refugees could have the power to reshape politics if granted full citizenship. Consider Lebanon and Jordan. In both countries, the refugee community makes up over 10 percent of the total population. This is part of the tension over how to grant refugees adequate rights and access to the state—the sheer numbers of them could have a significant impact with which many citizens are uncomfortable.

The refugee crisis is already changing the way politics are conducted, particularly in the European Union. Far-right parties have risen to prominence as anti-immigration sentiment becomes more widespread. And, if they are brought into power in countries like France and Denmark, these politicians could shape policy for decades to come. In the United Kingdom, anti-immigration sentiment helped contribute to their voting to leaving the European Union, the first country to do so since the European Union was founded after World War II. Policies that will affect refugees significantly, including new restrictions on resettlement, are also being introduced in legislatures.

WHAT TEEN REFUGEES NEED

The resources and services teen refugees need are a lot like the needs of teens anywhere. They need secure homes where they feel safe, nutritious food and clean water to stay healthy, and schools that allow them to grow their intellectual capabilities. But those needs are often unmet for refugees, and a lot of teenagers end up leaving school or home to take on adult responsibilities long before they turn eighteen.

Among the most pressing issues facing is a lack of documentation. This applies to young people trying to enroll in school and get access to services, as well as the organizations trying to help them. As we learned about in the last chapter, this is a particularly serious issue in Greece, where young people often lie about their ages in order to try making their way to

Somalian refugees at their school in Malaysia

Europe. When teenagers are uncared for, they can fall victim to crime or exploitation.

MENTAL HEALTH

Even before arriving in a refugee camp, most young people fleeing conflict or famine have experienced unthinkable things. According to research by the National Child Traumatic Stress Network, teenagers are extremely likely to have witnessed violence or been the victims of violence prior to leaving their countries of origin. The organization reported in the "Review of Child and Adolescent Refugee Mental Health" in 2003 that:

> In Mozambique, one study found that 77 percent of over five hundred children surveyed had witnessed murders or mass killings. Elsewhere, among a sample of forty adolescent Cambodian refugees who had survived four years in a Pol Pot "work camp," 98 percent endured forced labor, 90 percent lived in age segregated camps, and 83 percent lacked sufficient food for long periods of time.

These kinds of circumstances can lead to depression, grief, suicidal thoughts, post-traumatic stress disorder, aggression, or other behaviors that inhibit young people's ability to learn, grow, and thrive. While young people in refugee camps and communities sometimes have access to resources, including centers that allow them to express themselves and work through their experiences, many young people do not—including those who are living in cities without the infrastructure provided by groups like UNHCR. These young people are often burdened with trauma.

For many, the trauma does not stop whether or not they reach refugee camps. A study by UNICEF found that Syrians living outside of camps in Jordan are dealing with more stressors that negatively impact their mental well-being. According to a report by the UNHCR:

> Mental health findings reveal that Syrian refugee adolescents living in non-camp settings have more emotional distress, feel less supported, less safe, and have more perceived discrimination when compared to Zaatari refugee camp adolescents. They are also more scared to walk alone or to be away from parents.

POVERTY

Life as a refugee can have lasting damaging impact on teenagers. Although many have been able to resettle in new countries and adapt well, the experiences of many who are still living in refugee camps can impact their mental and physical health. An estimated nine out of ten refugees in Jordan live in poverty or are in danger of living in poverty. The overall number of Syrian refugees living in poverty has risen as high as 70 percent in countries like Turkey and Lebanon.

Years in poverty can lead to health problems, including high blood pressure later in life, and poverty often means a lack of access to healthy food and clean water. For teenagers who are still growing, this lack of access can cause even more severe health problems in the future. An article in the *Journal of the*

American Academy of Child and Adolescent Psychiatry explains the potential health impact some refugee children face:

> Cerebral malaria, meningitis, and encephalitis can cause permanent neurological and psychological [conditions]. Over time, acute malnutrition with its immediate health consequences ... often leads to chronic malnutrition that can impair immune function and increase susceptibility to infections (Dallman, 1987). Iron deficiency anemia causes lethargy and depression ...

Breaking the cycle of poverty that many refugees find themselves in is crucial to establishing stability. Pictured are refugees in Turkey.

Some young people have been the victims of extreme violence, which can leave lasting physical impairments, like untreated fractures of bones. To help combat these issues, young people need to be given access to clean water, food, and medical care as soon as possible after fleeing their home countries. They also need to be given resources to help them cope with issues that will have a lasting impact on their mobility, education, and other areas.

EDUCATION

Poverty also has negative consequences for access to education. Many teenagers are forced to leave school and take on jobs to help support their families, and young girls are at risk of being married at an early age in attempts to secure their economic future. In other cases, families are unable to pay school fees to enroll their children, resulting in lost years of education. Taking on jobs can be dangerous for young people, who are seen as easy to exploit. In Lebanon, sixteen-year-old Omar took a job washing dishes rather than going to school, with his mother telling Human Rights Watch:

> We can't afford to put them in school here. All my children were studying in Syria, but if I would put them in school here how would I live? We would have to buy them clothes and pay for transportation. Even if everything was free, the children couldn't go to school. They are the only ones that can work.

Even those who do have access to education are often unable to learn what they need to, and some drop out. According to

UNHCR, around 20 percent of Syrian children who enroll in schools in Lebanon eventually drop out, particularly among those over the age of twelve. This happens for a few reasons. One of them is that children are bullied by peers or teachers. UNICEF has reported that in the Zaatari camp in Jordan, children are verbally abused by teachers, with one seventeen-year-old girl telling them, "We can't get educated at the cost of self-respect. We fall victim to verbal abuse," including being told the children have ruined Jordan.

Other students have difficulty keeping up with lessons due to language barriers. In Lebanon, Syrian refugee Noura left school at age fourteen because instruction was difficult for her to understand. Her mother told Human Rights Watch that she and her younger brother "weren't learning in school, the curriculum was hard. They didn't understand the French. Noura got married two months ago."

Increasing access to education is one of the most critical steps in making sure refugee teenagers are able to live the lives they want. To do so, classes in basic language instruction are necessary, as are classes scheduled to make it easy for all students to attend—including those who are obliged to work jobs. Other barriers, like cost or restrictions on who can take classes, have to be reworked so that young people from all backgrounds are able to learn.

TEENAGERS MAKING A DIFFERENCE

Although life is difficult for teenage refugees, many have worked hard to make their voices heard and make a difference in their communities. There are also teens all over the world doing their part to help their refugee peers, from advocating for their rights to donating time or goods needed to make sure refugees are safe and cared for.

Natasha Maimba and Minahil Sarfraz are two teen refugees fighting for their fellow refugees. Natasha was eleven when she and her family fled Zimbabwe, while Minahil left Pakistan at age five. The two girls met when they were fourteen and fifteen, living in an asylum center in Ireland. Both were interested in activism and decided to join forces, helping each other overcome fear or doubt to get their shared message out. "If [Natasha] has the confidence to tell her story, then I feel that I'm confident as well, because we're the same age, based in similar situations," Minahil told Refinery29 in 2016. "It's pretty helpful to know that there's someone [with you] through the journey."

Natasha and Minahil are now Youth Ambassadors to UNICEF and speak around the world on behalf of refugee children. They regularly call on governments and organizations to do more to guarantee that refugee children not only receive the care they need, but also the respect, with Minahil saying, "Welcoming refugees, that can be a huge thing. I know if I was back to the time when I was young and I was all alone, I would have loved if somebody just came up to me and said, 'Hi, welcome.'" "It's up to us as young people to make sure we accommodate for change," Natasha said in the same interview.

Zeynab Ali is another refugee teen speaking out about her experiences. She was born in a refugee camp in Kenya after her parents fled Somalia. She has lived in the United States since she was six, but still faces hardship, particularly in light of the rise in anti-immigrant and refugee sentiment seen around the world. She has long been involved in her community in Milwaukee, Wisconsin, where she was awarded a Youth Leader Award in 2016 in recognition of her work in crime prevention. To combat misconceptions further, she wrote a book. It's called *Cataclysm: Secrets of the Horn of Africa,* a memoir and history of Somalia that she hopes will show people a different side of the refugee experience.

Another young woman changing the way the world sees teen refugees is Yusra Mardini, an Olympic swimmer who took part in the 2016 Rio Olympics as part of the world's first refugee team. Yusra fled Syria in 2015. While trying to make

The world's first refugee team—including teenagers—competed in the 2016 Rio Olympics.

it to Germany, she and her sister nearly drowned when they were on a boat that capsized. Yusra, a strong swimmer, helped bring the small vessel to shore through the dark, cold waters. "My story is hard, but it is not anything [compared to] other peoples' stories. Others lost their moms or their family and it's really hard. I am showing all the people that, yes, we are refugees, but we can do everything," she told *People*, which named her one of the twenty-five women changing the world in 2016.

Teens around the world are also helping refugees in any way they can. Groups like Fort Worth Youth International in Texas and Helping Our People Endure (HOPE) in London put teens front and center when it comes to planning and helping refugees. HOPE was founded by eighteen-year-old Amin, a teenager from Syria who has resettled in the UK. He began raising money for refugees after seeing the need in his own community. "I noticed that a lot of the aid provided to Syrian refugees was mainly focused towards food and shelter—there was no meaningful impact on education," he told the *Independent*. "These are children who haven't been in school for three, four years and no one's doing anything about it. There was a huge gap for aid and I saw it as an opportunity to step in and help. As a student, I truly see the benefit of education and how important it is. That's part of our philosophy."

Since starting the foundation in 2015, Amin has partnered with Lebanese organizations and raised thousands of dollars for Syrian families in Lebanon and funded scholarships for over sixty students. He said, "As a Syrian, the most hurtful thing for me to see is this lost generation—a generation that has lost five, six years of education. It truly pains me."

Teens 4 Refugees is an organization in the United States that helps organize donation drives and volunteer efforts for teenagers, as well as publishing letters and articles by teens who care about sharing refugee stories. According to their website, "you don't have to be over 21, have a license, be the president of UNESCO or be a writer to help. You just have to want to make a change."

RAYS OF HOPE

For millions of teenagers around the world, life has been disrupted by conflict that has forced them to flee their homes. In some cases, their lives are changed overnight as they have to leave behind their lives in order to find safety in another country, where they often do not find much comfort. The refugee crisis has had a profound impact on the globe already, shaping politics in the West and changing the demographics of countries where large refugee populations are being hosted. It is perhaps the most pressing issue facing the international community today.

Teenage refugees are faced with challenges that range from a lack of education to mental health concerns to difficulty meeting basic needs. Often, teenagers are forced to grow up quickly to help meet the needs of their families, either by caring for children, helping around the home, or working to bring in income. For unaccompanied teenagers, life is even more difficult as they work to avoid being exploited, abused, or lost in the shuffle of countries overwhelmed by the refugee crisis.

More and more, people are coming to understand the toll being taken on an entire generation of young people from Syria,

HOW TO GET INVOLVED

Teens around the world are leading the way in helping refugees, and it's easy to get involved with the efforts. It's even possible to help out from your own home! Here are a few ideas on how to help out:

- Organize a fundraiser for UNICEF, Save the Children, or another organization helping young refugees.
- Start a donation drive for refugees in Greece, who need warm winter coats and other goods.
- Work with a teacher to make a presentation to share more about the refugee crisis with your peers.
- Raise awareness by talking to your friends or starting a letter writing campaign to your local representatives.
- Reach out to local refugee organizations to learn more about volunteering. Organizations like Girl Up have chapters around the country, while local communities and churches often have resettlement programs that rely on volunteer support.
- If you have refugees in your school, make an effort to get to know them and make them feel welcome.
- Stay informed by following the latest news on the refugee crisis—knowing what's going on is an important step in finding a way you can help out!

Iraq, Yemen, Sudan, and other countries facing war, famine, or natural disasters. While progress is being made to meet the needs of these young people, there remains much to be done by governments and international organizations. In order to help teenage refugees and ensure that they are able to live up to their potential, everyone must come together and make sure these adolescents are being taken care of. Until then, millions will continue to struggle every day.

GLOSSARY

Abou Shouk A large refugee camp in Darfur, housing internally displaced persons.

Adolescent-Friendly Spaces (AFS) Special centers with classes, activities, and other resources for teenagers.

"the berm" A desert area between Syria and Jordan where thousands of refugees are housed despite adverse conditions.

Calais migrant camp A large migrant and refugee camp on the coast of France, housing thousands of asylum seekers and others seeking the right to settle in Europe or the United Kingdom.

Convention of the Rights of the Child An international agreement outlining the recognized rights of those under the age of eighteen.

detention center A large building, often with limited privacy, where people are housed temporarily while waiting for resettlement or other housing options.

displaced persons People forced to flee their homes due to threats to their life. Internally displaced persons remain in their country of origin.

drop-in centers School facilities that offer flexible learning opportunities so students with difficult schedules can attend classes or meet with instructors whenever they are free.

ethnic cleansing Forcing a specific group to leave a country or area by the use of violence or forced migration.

famine A long-term, extreme lack of food, which can be caused by drought or other disasters.

genocide The purposeful and targeted extermination of a single ethnic, religious, racial or other group.

in exile Living outside of one's country of origin.

Janjaweed Militias in Darfur that have taken an active and primary role in the country's ongoing genocide.

League of Nations A precursor to the United Nations, founded after World War I.

mandate Authority to oversee or do something, such as the UNHCR mandate to assist international refugees.

migrant A person who leaves their home country by choice to find work in another country.

nationality A legal status within a country that grants certain rights and privileges.

protracted refugee situations A country or region with a refugee population of at least twenty-five thousand people for longer than five years.

radicalization The process by which an individual is gradually encouraged to accept extremist ideology.

refugee A person forced to flee their home country due to threats to their life, such as war or persecution.

refugee camps Temporary spaces set up to house refugees in tents or other structures, featuring resources to help them while they are waiting for resettlement.

refugee status An approval process governed by countries that grants individuals certain rights, including the right to remain in that specific country.

resettlement The process by which refugees are granted the right to live and work in a specific country.

Six Grave Violations Against Children During Armed Conflict
Internationally recognized actions that inflict undue pain or
suffering on children.

smugglers People who use illegal routes to transport people
across countries, often for a large sum of money.

trauma Events and experiences that have a lingering impact
on one's mental or physical health.

unaccompanied children Minors who do not have a
parent or guardian with them when they arrive in a host
community.

UNICEF A United Nations agency that oversees efforts to aid
children.

United Nations High Commissioner for Refugees (UNHCR)
A United Nations organization that oversees efforts to help
refugees around the world, including running most refugee
camps.

Zaatari A large refugee camp in Jordan, housing more than
eighty thousand Syrian refugees.

Books

Jones, Reece. *Violent Borders: Refugees and the Right to Move.* London, UK: Verso, 2016.

Kingsley, Patrick. *The New Odyssey.* New York: Liveright, 2017.

Rawlence, Ben. *City of Thorns: Nine Lives in the World's Largest Refugee Camp.* New York: Picador, 2017.

Websites

Human Rights Watch
http://www. hrw.org
Human Rights Watch is an international human rights group that closely monitors the rights of children and adolescents in refugee settings. On their website find breaking news, reports on human rights situations around the world, and suggestions for how to help ensure that everyone is afforded basic care and dignity.

International Rescue Committee
http://www.rescue.org
Learn more about this international organization responding to major global crises, including those that impact or create refugee situations and get involved.

Refugees International

http://www.refugeesinternational.org

Find news and photo and video reports from this advocacy group that works on refugee-related policies around the world.

Videos

"Syria: The World's Largest Refugee Crisis - Full Episode"

https://www.youtube.com/watch?v=EEQdVSWvWWA

The Foreign Policy Association presents an information-packed documentary about the Syrian refugee crisis.

"Understanding the Refugee Crisis in Europe, Syria, and Around the World"

https://www.youtube.com/watch?v=KVV6_1Sef9M

John Green provides an overview of today's most pressing refugee crisis, providing statistics, context, and an empathetic look at refugees themselves.

Amnesty International. "Female Refugees Face Physical Assault, Exploitation, and Sexual Harassment on Their Journey through Europe." January 18, 2016. https://www.amnesty.org/en/latest/news/2016/01/female-refugees-face-physical-assault-exploitation-and-sexual-harassment-on-their-journey-through-europe/.

Braunschweiger, Amy. "Witness: A Child Soldier's Darfur Confession—'I Shot Her. She Is Dead.'" Human Rights Watch, September 9, 2015. https://www.hrw.org/news/2015/09/09/witness-child-soldiers-darfur-confession-i-shot-her-she-dead.

Connor, Phillip, and Jens Manuel Krogstad. "Key Facts About the World's Refugees." Pew Research Center, October 5, 2016. http://www.pewresearch.org/fact-tank/2016/10/05/key-facts-about-the-worlds-refugees/.

Corner, Lena. "Teenage Refugees Tell Us the Horrors They Went Through to Get to Europe." VICE, May 6, 2016. https://www.vice.com/en_uk/article/unaccompanied-refugee-minors-young-people-crisis.

Doctors Without Borders. "Without Freedom I Cannot Dream: An Afghan Refugee in Greece." June 19, 2013. http://www.doctorswithoutborders.org/news-stories/voice-field/without-freedom-i-cannot-dream-afghan-refugee-greece.

Dunmore, Charlie. "A Teenager Refugee Champions Girls' Education." UNHCR Tracks, November 25, 2015. http://tracks.unhcr.org/2015/11/a-teenage-refugee-champions-girls-education/.

Gentleman, Amelia. "Help Refugees: A Lifeline for Teenagers Living in Seedy Athens Squats." *The Guardian,* December 16, 2016. https://www.theguardian.com/society/2016/dec/16/help-refugees-charity-central-athens-vulnerable-young-people.

Human Rights Watch. "Growing Up Without an Education." July 19, 2016. https://www.hrw.org/report/2016/07/19/growing-without-education/barriers-education-syrian-refugee-children-.

Judd, Nicole. "Security Now: Addressing the Needs of Darfur's Children." University of Denver, Human Rights and Human Welfare Topical Research Digest. http://www.du.edu/korbel/hrhw/researchdigest/minority/Darfur.pdf.

Oxfam International. "Life in Za'atari Refugee Camp, Jordan's Fourth Biggest City." 2016. https://www.oxfam.

org/en/crisis-syria/life-zaatari-refugee-camp-jordans-fourth-biggest-city.

Peterson, Lilli. "These Inspiring Teenage Besties Are the New Face of the Refugee Crisis." Refinery 29, September 22, 2016. http://www.du.edu/korbel/hrhw/researchdigest/minority/Darfur.pdf.

Pierson, Elizabeth. "He Was 28, I Was 13: The Stories of Syrian Child Brides." Mashable, March 31, 2016. http://mashable.com/2016/03/31/syrian-child-brides/.

Riddell, Rebecca. "The Tragedy of Greece's Refugee Children." Human Rights Watch, September 9, 2016. https://www.hrw.org/news/2016/09/09/tragedy-greeces-refugee-children.

Spyridaki, Marina. "Greece: 'At Home We Had War, But At Least We Had Dignity.'" Doctors Without Borders, September 18, 2015. http://www.doctorswithoutborders.org/article/greece-home-we-had-war-least-we-had-dignity.

United Nations High Commissioner for Refugees. "Mental Health Psychosocial and Child Protection for Syrian Adolescent Refugees in Jordan." December, 2014. https://data2.unhcr.org/en/documents/details/42632.

———. "UNHCR Reports Crisis in Refugee Education." September 15, 2016. http://www.unhcr.org/afr/news/press/2016/9/57d7d6f34/unhcr-reports-crisis-refugee-education.html.

UNRWA. "Insights into the Socioeconomic Conditions of Palestinian Refugees in Jordan." 2013. https://www.unrwa.org/resources/reports/insights-socio-economic-conditions-palestinian-refugees-jordan.

Yardley, Jim. "A High Degree of Miserable in a Refugee Swollen Greece." *The New York Times*, March 17, 2016.

INDEX

Bridey Heing is a writer and book critic based in Washington, DC. She holds degrees in political science and international affairs from DePaul University and Washington University in Saint Louis. Her areas of focus are comparative politics and Iranian politics. Her master's thesis explores the evolution of populist politics and democracy in Iran since 1900. She has written about Iranian affairs, women's rights, and art and politics for publications like the *Economist, Hyperallergic*, and the *Establishment*. She also writes about literature and film. She enjoys traveling, reading, and exploring Washington's many museums.